# ONE-MINUTE STORIES OF GREAT AMERICANS

# ONE-MINUTE STORIES OF GREAT AMERICANS

Adapted by
## SHARI LEWIS
Research by Gerry Matthews

Illustrated by
## ROBERT BARRETT

DOUBLEDAY
New York   London   Toronto   Sydney   Auckland

*j 920.073 L*

PUBLISHED BY DOUBLEDAY
a division of Bantam Doubleday Dell Publishing Group, Inc.
666 Fifth Avenue, New York, New York 10103

DOUBLEDAY and the portrayal of an anchor
with a dolphin are trademarks of Doubleday,
a division of Bantam Doubleday Dell
Publishing Group, Inc.

Library of Congress Cataloging-in-Publication Data
Lewis, Shari.
One-minute great Americans / by Shari Lewis; research by Gerry Matthews.
p.     cm.
Summary: Twenty biographical sketches of inspirational figures in United
States history designed for reading in one minute or less. Includes George
Washington, Susan B. Anthony, Martin Luther King, Jr.,
Helen Keller, and others.
1. United States—Biography—Juvenile literature.   [1. United States—
Biography.   2. Biography.]   I. Matthews, Gerry.   II. Title.
CT217.L5   1990
920.073—dc20
[B]
[920]   89-30466   CIP   AC
Rl: 3.8
ISBN 0-385-24448-7

Printed in Italy
0990

# Contents

Introduction                                            6

Christopher Columbus                                    8

Captain John Smith and Pocahontas                      10

George Washington                                      12

Benjamin Franklin                                      14

Paul Revere                                            16

Thomas Jefferson                                       18

Meriwether Lewis and William Clark                     20

Andrew Jackson                                         22

Abraham Lincoln                                        24

Robert E. Lee                                          26

Clara Barton                                           28

Sitting Bull and Crazy Horse                           30

Theodore Roosevelt                                     32

The Wright Brothers                                    34

Susan B. Anthony                                       36

Thomas Edison                                          38

Helen Keller and Anne Sullivan                         40

George Washington Carver                               42

John Glenn and Neil Armstrong                          44

Dr. Martin Luther King, Jr.                            46

# Introduction

A history book for preschoolers and early graders?

Oh yes! Little children love stories, and that's what history is—his-story and her-story. Introducing the adventures of Thomas Edison or Abraham Lincoln, George Washington Carver or Clara Barton to a young child is a fine way to guarantee a more receptive student in the years to come.

History in one-minute bites?

Oh, yes! This One-Minute form is uniquely suited to the concentration spans of today's youngsters. It gives little ones about as much detail as they can absorb in a sitting. If you see that your child is intrigued by a particular hero or heroine of history, I urge you to seize the opportunity to turn to one of the children's encyclopedias and read on!

These Great Americans were only human, and their yearnings, their successes and failures are the stuff from which good yarns can be spun. Their life stories are not at all stuffy, unless they're pompously presented as "serious" material.

As I adapted these biographies, I was shocked at the surge of power I experienced; I never realized that as you write a history book, you rewrite history. When you select the individuals to be featured, you *must* make choices. You pick events and anecdotes and in selecting, you change the perspectives of the past.

As much as I wanted to, I couldn't avoid the emphasis on military heroes, for military victories have made America's survival possible—but I've also presented heroes of culture, invention, exploration, and medicine. I didn't want kids to feel that the only way glory could be achieved, or perceived, was through the barrel of a gun.

I've tried to include Great Americans of varied social, economic, and ethnic backgrounds. So this is a book about men of intellect, warmth, and wisdom, as well as men of war. Mostly, it *is* about men. As women more evenly share the events of the generations ahead, history books will be better balanced. But this is history, not fantasy, and I've dealt with what has come before, not what will be.

Shari Lewis

## Christopher Columbus
### (1451–1506)

IN 1451, Christopher Columbus was born in Italy. Many people then believed that the earth was flat. They said that if a ship went too far, it would fall right off the edge. Tales were told of terrible sea monsters that could swallow a ship in just one bite.

In those days, the only way to get the beautiful silks and wonderful spices that everyone wanted was to travel to India and the East—but it took a long time to get there by land, and even longer to sail south around the bottom of Africa and *then* sail east, toward India. The person who could find a new and faster way to get to those far-off lands would become rich.

Christopher Columbus felt that the world was round, not flat. He was convinced that the shortest way to reach India was to sail west, right toward what other people considered the end of the earth. After all, he thought, if the world is indeed a ball, and you sail straight ahead of you, eventually you must come around to the other side, and there would be India and the East!

8

He went to the kings of England, France, and Portugal and told them of his plan. No one believed him. But the Spanish King Ferdinand and Queen Isabella gave him money for three ships: The *Niña*, the *Pinta*, and the *Santa Maria*, and off he sailed. What Columbus did not know was that he would be stopped from arriving in India by a whole other continent that nobody even knew existed!

On October 12, 1492, Columbus and his crew landed on an island off the coast of what would soon be called America. They went ashore, and Columbus claimed this New World for Spain.

Captain John Smith
(1580–1631)
and
Pocahontas
(1595?–1617)

IN 1606, Captain John Smith left a safe, comfortable life in England and came to America with a tiny group of brave people. They built cabins of logs and mud and named their village Jamestown, after their king, James I.

The crops they planted didn't grow and the colonists almost starved, so John Smith decided to ask the Indians for help. Indians had lived in America for thousands of years and they knew how to grow corn and catch turkeys and deer for meat.

However, the Indians were afraid of the strange, pale-faced people who had sailed across the sea and moved onto Indian lands.

So when Captain John Smith walked into the Indian camp, he was taken prisoner. While there, he met the chief's twelve-year-old daughter, who was called Pocahontas, which means "playful." Each day the girl would visit John, and he would tell her stories of his home far across the sea. It is said that Pocahontas fell in love with John Smith.

The Indian chief, Powhatan, had decided to kill the captain as a warning to others in Jamestown, but Pocahontas stopped him. She said the Indians would have to kill *her* before they could kill the Captain. Powhatan gave in. He got to know John Smith and they became friends.

When Pocahontas was older, she married one of the settlers. She even went to England and met King James!

# George Washington
## (1732–1799)

MANY people sailed from Great Britain to the New World. They built their homes in thirteen settlements called colonies, which were ruled by the British king. When George Washington was growing up, he lived in Virginia, one of the original colonies.

Life in America was not easy, for these were mainly unexplored lands, filled with Indians and wild animals.

The Indians, who were afraid of the colonists, sometimes burned the colonists' homes. Occasionally the British settlers were attacked by the French who lived nearby, in Canada. That is why King James I sent soldiers to protect his British subjects in America.

As a young man, George Washington was put in charge of some of the soldiers, and he spent years in the wilderness.

Americans had to pay taxes to the British king, for he was their ruler. But the taxes became so high that the settlers couldn't afford them, and they refused to pay. At a meeting called the Continental

Congress, the colonists wrote the Declaration of Independence, telling the king that they wanted to run America themselves.

Congress made George Washington the general of the American Army, and the British and Americans fought the War of Independence, which is also called the American Revolution.

The British had never battled in wilderness like America, but Washington's army had learned that type of fighting from the Indians, so even though there were many more British soldiers than there were Americans, George Washington's army won the war.

Then the colonists wanted General George Washington to become the king of America, but he didn't believe that our country should *have* a king. Instead, he became the first President of the United States of America.

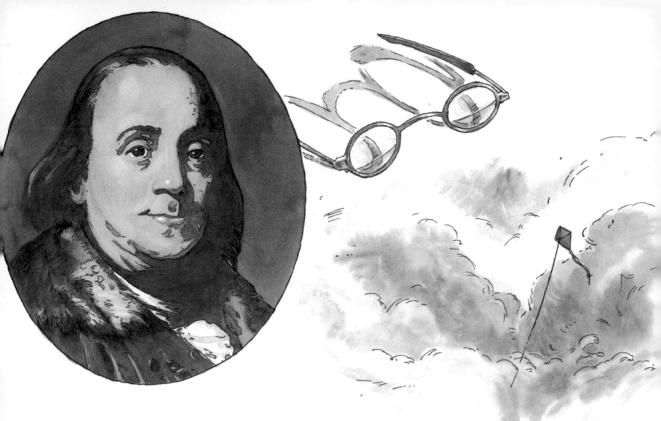

## Benjamin Franklin

### (1706–1790)

BENJAMIN Franklin was so poor that he had to leave school at the age of ten. When he was seventeen, he became a printer in Philadelphia and eventually published his own newspaper called *Poor Richard's Almanack*, in which he printed sayings that we still use, like "Early to bed, early to rise, makes a man healthy, wealthy and wise."

But Benjamin Franklin didn't just *say* wonderful things. He *did* amazing things as well.

He started the first public library in America. The first city post office. The first fire department in Philadelphia. The first city hospital. He invented bifocal eyeglasses, in which each lens is divided in half: When you look through the top half, you can see far into the distance, and when you look through the bottom half, it helps you to see things that are close up. People wear bifocals to this very day.

And one stormy night, Benjamin Franklin flew a kite into a thundercloud. A metal key on the kite was attached to a long wire, held by Ben. When lightning struck the key, sparks ran down the wire, giving Franklin quite a shock, but proving for the first time that lightning was electricity. Then Ben Franklin invented the lightning rod, which has saved many homes from being destroyed by lightning.

Before our War of Independence, Mr. Franklin traveled to Great Britain to ask the king to let American colonists rule themselves. The king wouldn't listen, and when the Revolutionary War started, Franklin went to France and persuaded the French to help America win.

After the war, Benjamin Franklin helped write the Constitution of the United States of America, which is the group of laws by which we still live today.

# Paul Revere
## (1735–1818)

LISTEN, my children, and you shall hear
Of the midnight ride of Paul Revere.

Paul Revere was both a silversmith and an engraver, but it was a horseback ride that made him famous.

The night the American War of Independence started, the British were coming to capture the city of Boston and take away the American colonists' guns and supplies. No one knew from which direction the soldiers would attack.

Paul Revere arranged for a friend to go into a high church tower, where he could see what was going on all around Boston. If the British attacked by land, he would light one lantern. He would light two lanterns if they were sailing to attack.

The British came by sea.

After the two lanterns were lit, Paul Revere got on his horse.

He called "To arms!" all along his ride,
"The British are coming on the morning tide!"

He woke the Americans from their deep sleep, and the colonists were ready and able to surprise the British soldiers when they attacked. Thanks to Paul Revere's warning, the colonists won that battle.

And that is why today we cheer
The midnight ride of Paul Revere.

## Thomas Jefferson
### (1743–1826)

WHEN Thomas Jefferson was fourteen years old, his father died and he became head of his family, with six sisters and a brother to take care of. In spite of this heavy responsibility, Tom went to college and became a lawyer. When he was elected to the government of Virginia, he worked with the other patriots trying to get Britain to let Americans run the country by themselves.

At a meeting of the first Continental Congress, the other patriots were so impressed with what Jefferson knew about history and law, they asked him to write the Declaration of Independence, which explains in a wonderful way what our country stands for. It says that nobody is better than anybody else, and that the right to be free and happy shouldn't be taken away from anyone. It also says Americans will not bow down to the king or pay taxes to him, which caused the Revolutionary War to begin.

Jefferson was Governor of Virginia during the war, and afterward he worked as President Washington's Secretary of State.

Then, in 1800, Jefferson became the third President of the United States, and held office for eight years.

## Meriwether Lewis and William Clark
### (1774–1809) (1770–1838)

WHEN Thomas Jefferson was President, he asked Captain Meriwether Lewis and William Clark to travel across the northern part of America to find a safe way to get to the Pacific Ocean. With a group of brave men, they went by boat from St. Louis up the Missouri River into wilderness that had never been explored. They spent the winter with the Indians in North Dakota, then hiked on until the high Rocky Mountains blocked their way. Luckily their Indian guide, a woman named Sacajawea, got horses for them from other Indians,

and they rode over the mountains until they came to a river flowing west.

The travelers built new boats right on the spot, and paddled until they got to the Pacific Ocean.

They thought the government was going to send a ship to bring them home, but no ship came, so they split up into two groups and set off in two different directions to explore and make maps of as much of the West as they could. One man died, but the rest arrived back in Missouri after three years of paddling canoes and walking through dangerous Indian territory.

Lewis and Clark were the very first explorers to make maps of the land surrounding what is now the State of Oregon, and they helped the people of the original thirteen states realize how important those western lands really are.

## Andrew Jackson
### (1767–1845)

ANDREW Jackson was born in a log cabin on the South Carolina frontier after his father had died. He lost his mother when he was only fourteen. He fought in the Revolution, and then became a lawyer. In the War of 1812, when the British attacked America for the second time, Jackson led an army that defeated the enemy in the Battle of New Orleans.

The common working people loved Jackson because he had started out as a poor country boy and understood their problems. They nicknamed him "Old Hickory" because he was tall and strong, and they elected him seventh President of the United States.

The new President rode to Washington, D.C., on horseback, and stayed at a tavern until the White House was fixed up so he could

move in. Farmers and frontiersmen came from all over to see their hero.

After Jackson was sworn in as President, the White House became so crowded with happy country folk that Old Hickory had to climb out of a rear window and sneak back to the tavern to get a little privacy and a good night's sleep before taking on the very difficult job of being President.

# Abraham Lincoln
## (1809–1865)

ABRAHAM Lincoln's mother died when he was small. His father was a farmer and carpenter who never made much money. Little Abe went to school for only one year, but he had a few books and taught himself by reading them over and over again, with only the light of the fireplace.

As he was growing up, Abe's first job was splitting logs for fence rails. Then he opened a grocery store. Young Mr. Lincoln's honesty and good spirits made everyone like him, but he wasn't good at business. After his store failed, he worked as a postmaster and then as a surveyor, without much luck. But during those hard times Abe kept studying, and he finally became a lawyer. At last, Abe Lincoln had found something at which he was really good.

Abe got involved in politics, and right before the Civil War began, he was elected sixteenth President of the United States. The war between the North and the South was fought to end slavery in this country, and one evening, just before the war was won by the North, President Lincoln took his wife out to celebrate. That night, while watching a play in Ford's Theatre in Washington, D.C., Abraham Lincoln was killed by an actor named John Wilkes Booth, who mistakenly thought that by killing the President, he was helping the cause of the South.

## Robert E. Lee
### (1807–1870)

ROBERT E. Lee was trained as a soldier at West Point. He graduated second in his class and became an officer in the United States Army.

When the Civil War began between the Northern and Southern states, he was asked to be commander of the Union army of the North, but Robert E. Lee's family was from Virginia and his heart was with the South, so he became the general in charge of the Southern Confederate Army.

In those days, officers rode on horseback. General Lee's horse, named Traveller, could outrun most other horses in the army. Horses were often frightened by the blasts of guns, but not Traveller. It is said that Traveller reared into the air only once, and that was to let a cannonball pass under his belly; if he hadn't, both he and the general would have been killed.

In spite of his wise leadership, General Robert E. Lee's Confederate Army lost the Civil War, and the North and South were reunited once and for all.

General Lee said, "I shall devote my remaining energies to training young men to do their duty in life," and he became president of Washington College in Lexington, Virginia.

## Clara Barton
### (1821–1912)

DURING the Civil War, a country schoolteacher named Clara Barton offered to help care for wounded soldiers. She risked her life in the battlefields, bringing bandages and medicines to the injured and dying men. Grateful Union soldiers called her the Angel of the Battlefield. Before the war was over, Clara was in charge of all the hospitals for the North.

After the war, President Lincoln asked Miss Barton to lead the search for the many Union soldiers still missing.

When her work in America was finished, Clara Barton went to Europe to serve as a nurse in the Franco-Prussian War, between France and Germany. There she learned about the International Red Cross, a group of people who took care of soldiers right where the fighting was taking place. Impressed with the way the Red Cross worked in Europe, Clara Barton started the same type of organization in America. It took several years, but she finally received approval from the President of the United States. Now our Red Cross helps people not only during wars, but when there are floods, earthquakes, and other disasters.

Thanks to Clara Barton, the American Red Cross is always there to help.

## Sitting Bull  and  Crazy Horse
### (1834–1890)       (1849?–1877)

AMERICANS needed new land for farms and homes, so they moved west onto the Great Plains, chasing off the Indians who already lived there. To make room for their cattle, the farmers and ranchers killed huge herds of buffalo, which the Indians needed for meat and clothing.

When angry Indians went on the warpath, the United States Army was sent to chase the Indians away. At that time there were two great Indian leaders, both chiefs of the Sioux tribe. Their names were Crazy Horse and Sitting Bull. Crazy Horse was known for his daring in battle, while Sitting Bull was considered a wise Indian leader and medicine man.

In a battle against United States soldiers, Sitting Bull and Crazy Horse led the largest gathering of Indians on horseback in American history. At a place called Little Big Horn, they killed all the soldiers, including the colonel, George Armstrong Custer.

Since Custer had been a hero in the Civil War, his death made Americans angry. In their anger, they forgot that the Indians had a right to defend their land and their lives, so Crazy Horse was killed in prison. Sitting Bull escaped to Canada, but returned in a few years. He never fought again, but Chief Sitting Bull spent the rest of his life working for Indian people's rights.

## Theodore Roosevelt
### (1858–1919)

LITTLE Teddy Roosevelt wasn't very strong.

His eyes were weak and his knees were knobby,
He couldn't go to school and he didn't have a hobby
So he stayed at home. Worked on his muscles,
Ate good food for his red corpuscles.
He became strong. He became tough.
As for horseback riding, he couldn't get enough.
He said, "When I grow to be a man,
I'll join the army as fast as I can."

And he did!

The Rough Riders were his regiment.
They rode well, so they were sent
To Cuba to get rid of Spain.
He fought so fiercely, it was plain
This powerful fellow wanted to be
The leader of the people in the Land of the Free.
He became President in 1901.
He said, "Bully, bully, this is fun!"
For Theodore Roosevelt, it was so nice
Being President, he did it twice.

## THE WRIGHT BROTHERS
### Orville and Wilbur
#### (1871–1948)    (1867–1912)

ORVILLE and Wilbur Wright had always tinkered with gadgets and mechanical inventions. They built a printing press, and a few years later designed and made bicycles. Then the brothers took an interest in creating an airplane.

All over the world, scientists and inventors were trying to make a machine in which a person could fly. There were big balloons that could carry a couple of people up in a basket, but there was no way to control which way the balloon went once it was up in the sky. The wind might even blow it out to sea or into a mountain.

The Wright brothers began to design kites and gliders, and then they added a little gasoline engine and propeller to their glider.

At a windy beach in North Carolina called Kitty Hawk, on December 17, 1903, Orville Wright made the first flight in an airplane. It lasted fifty-nine seconds, and six people saw him do it: his brother Wilbur and five Coast Guardsmen. The Wright brothers had chosen Kitty Hawk because it was the windiest place they could find, and the wind helped keep the plane up in the air.

Only one newspaper carried the story, for no one could believe the Wright brothers. They had done something no one had ever done before: They had put a motor into something that was heavier than air, and it had flown.

## Susan B. Anthony
### (1820–1906)

SUSAN Brownell Anthony was quite a woman! She saw things that were wrong in the world around her, and worked all of her life to change them.

When Susan B. Anthony was a girl, women in our country were thought of as less important than men, and certainly less intelligent. Men ran the world, while women watched. A woman could not go to college. If she worked, she was paid very little money. And women were not allowed to vote.

In Rochester, New York, in 1872, Susan B. Anthony led a group of women who tried to vote. She was arrested and went to court, where she lost her case. But she would win in the end.

"Suffrage" is a word that means "the right to vote." That's why Susan B. Anthony named her organization The National Woman Suffrage Organization, whose members became known as "Suffragettes." They fought for women's rights, and in 1920 it became the law of the land: Women were given the right to vote!

In 1978, Ms. Anthony's face appeared on a silver dollar. Susan B. Anthony has the honor of being the first woman in history to be pictured on any kind of American money.

## Thomas Edison
### (1847–1931)

TOM Edison went to school for only three months, but his mother taught him at home. By the time he was twelve, he was selling newspapers in order to raise money for his scientific experiments. He was a natural inventor and would often get the idea for something brand-new that no one had ever thought of.

Edison created the first electric lamp. He built the first electric plant in the world, which supplied electricity for New York City and the surrounding areas.

He invented the gramophone machine, which later developed into the phonograph, hi-fi, and stereo.

While still a young man, Edison sold his inventions for lots of money and set up a laboratory in New Jersey where other talented scientists working with him turned out new inventions by the dozen. They developed the first motion picture process, which he called "an optical phonograph" (which really means a phonograph record you can see). And having invented the way to watch pictures move on the screen, the Edison company went into the movie business and made motion pictures.

Edison liked playing at his work so much, he often forgot to stop, even for meals or to sleep.

Thomas A. Edison was probably the most inventive man of his time. The world would not be the same if he had not been in it!

## Helen Keller
(1880–1968)
and
Anne Sullivan
(1866–1936)

BEFORE she was two years old, Helen Keller became blind and deaf from a serious illness. She turned into a wild child, throwing her food and breaking things. Her parents hired Anne Sullivan to live with Helen and teach her to get along in the world.

Since Helen couldn't see or hear, Anne Sullivan had to teach her by touch. She would spell the words out in sign language with her fingers, right onto the palm of Helen's hand.

40

One day, she taught Helen the word "water" by pouring water over the child's hand and then spelling the word out onto her palm. Helen was smart. She suddenly understood, and a new and wonderful world opened up to her. No longer alone in her darkness, she had a friend with whom she could talk.

And Helen wanted to know everything.

Feeling vibrations in her teacher's throat as Anne spoke, Helen learned how to make the right sounds and say words with her own voice. She graduated from university, wrote books, and gave talks on how hard it was to be blind, but how good it was to be alive.

If a hero is someone who is brave and doesn't let anyone stop him or her from doing what needs to be done, there's no question about it —Helen Keller was a hero.

## George Washington Carver
### (1864–1943)

BORN a slave during the Civil War, young George Washington Carver was a scientific genius. But even after the war, when blacks were supposed to be treated equally, he had a hard time finding a college that would let him in. When he did, he was such a wonderful student, they asked Mr. Carver to stay and teach other students.

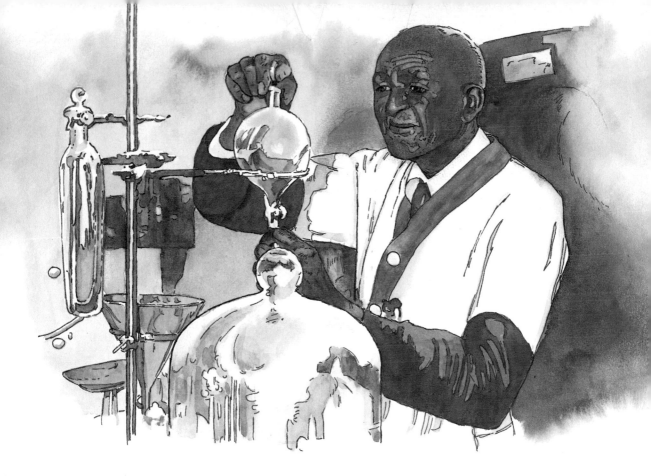

Later he went to Tuskegee Institute in Alabama, where for forty-seven years he tried to find ways to help farmers, particularly black farmers of the South. He taught them not to plant cotton every year —that causes the soil to get used up. "Instead," he said, "plant peanuts one year, soybeans the next, cotton the third year, and then start again with a crop of peanuts. It's called crop rotation." Farmers everywhere have practiced crop rotation ever since.

George Washington Carver worked hard to discover ways to grow peanuts that made them taste even better. He went to Washington, D.C., and told the people in Congress what he had discovered. But in spite of his fame, Carver wasn't allowed to eat in a white restaurant or stay overnight in a white hotel. It was 1921, and black people were still treated as second-class citizens, even in the capital of the United States. In Europe, however, George Washington Carver was honored as the great man he was, and today we are all proud to remember him as an American hero.

# John Glenn
## (1921–    )
## and
## Neil Armstrong
## (1930–    )

JOHN Glenn and Neil Armstrong were the first two Americans to become heroes in outer space.

John Glenn won many medals for bravery as a fighter pilot in both World War II and the Korean War.

Then Glenn became the first test pilot to fly faster than the speed of sound across the United States. For the American space program, in 1962, John Glenn was the very first astronaut to go around the earth in a space capsule.

Neil Armstrong grew up building model airplanes, dreaming of the day he'd be able to fly real ones. After college, Armstrong was such a daring and successful pilot, he became an astronaut, too.

In 1969, Neil Armstrong flew to the moon and landed there in a lunar module called *The Eagle.*

Nearly everyone on earth who had a TV set watched as Armstrong climbed down a ladder and was the first man to step onto the surface of the moon. "That's one small step for man," he said, "one giant leap for mankind."

## Dr. Martin Luther King, Jr.
### (1929–1968)

DR. Martin Luther King, Jr., was the most important leader of the Civil Rights movement in the 1960s.

At that time, black citizens in many American cities had to live in all-black neighborhoods, eat in all-black restaurants, and sit in the back of buses and movie theaters. Black children couldn't even go to school with white youngsters.

There were many jobs blacks were simply not allowed to have.

Dr. King helped organize peaceful demonstrations to object to the way his people were being treated. He bravely led thousands of people in protest marches, and gave stirring speeches asking the citizens of the United States to understand that in a democracy like ours, all people are equal.

He and his father were often treated badly by white bullies. They were spat upon, shot at, and arrested. King's house was blown up, and the FBI tried to prove that he was an enemy of our country.

But Martin Luther King, Jr., had a dream of a loving world. He said, "We must love our white brothers, no matter what they do to us." He was awarded the Nobel Peace Prize, a great honor presented every year to the person who does the most to bring about peace in the world.

Sadly, at the age of thirty-nine, long before his work was finished, Martin Luther King, Jr., was shot and killed. A great voice was silenced, but in his name the fight for justice and equal opportunity for black people goes on.

We now celebrate Martin Luther King Day as a national holiday on the second Monday in January.